Delicates

WENDY GUERRA

Delicates

TRANSLATED BY NANCY NAOMI CARLSON

AND ESPERANZA HOPE SNYDER

LONDON NEW YORK CALCUTTA

Seagull Books, 2023

Originally published in Spanish as *Ropa interior* by Bruguera, Barcelona
© Wendy Guerra, 2008

First published in English translation by Seagull Books, 2023
English translation © Nancy Naomi Carlson and Esperanza Hope Snyder, 2023

ISBN   978 1 8030 9 166 2

British Library Cataloguing-in-Publication Data
A catalogue record for this book is available from the British Library

Typeset by Seagull Books, Calcutta, India
Printed and bound by WordsWorth India, New Delhi, India

The editor returned my book, saying:
"Madam, take away all your undergarments,
your book doesn't interest us . . ."

Anaïs Nin, *Letters*

She turns and looks a moment in the glass,
Hardly aware of her departed lover;
Her brain allows one half-formed thought to pass:
"Well now that's done: and I'm glad it's over."
When lovely woman stoops to folly and
Paces about her room again, alone,
She smoothes her hair with automatic hand
And puts a record on the gramophone.

T. S. Eliot, *The Waste Land*

I was the guardian of absence
and memory could not be lost to me . . .

Reina María Rodríguez, *Collected Works*

CONTENTS

TRANSLATORS' FOREWORD • *ix*

Peninsular Psalm • **3**

Red • **5**

Snow in Havana • **6**

Winter Sports • **8**

Salt • **9**

Traveling in Reverse • **10**

A Face in the Crowd (Graffiti) • **11**

Memory and Dust • **12**

News from the Queen • **13**

Closed Season on Manatees • **14**

Inuit Promise • **16**

Vertigo Over the Niagara • **17**

Delicates • **18**

Breaking Crystal Dragonflies • **20**

Kaos Is Written with a K • **21**

The Actress • **23**

Naughty Girl • **24**

Ideas for Silhouettes • **25**

Last Apocrypha of Ana Mendieta • **26**

Possible Similes • **28**

Subway Map • **29**

Promenade through the Private Museum • **30**

Orgy of the Wind • **31**

Jazz Trio • **32**

The Prince and the Pauper • **34**

The Year It Snows • **35**

Airport • **36**

From Pompeii • **37**

Far Away Like Cuba • **38**

Curatorship • **40**

Vertical Psalm • **41**

On Your Knees • **42**

Excess Baggage • **43**

Consulted Archives • **44**

Without Salvation • **45**

A Cabala of Cast-offs • **47**

Touché • **48**

Razor to the Wind • **49**

Living on the Airwaves • **50**

On How the Russians Started Saying Goodbye • **51**

Déclassée • **52**

Sea of Tears • **53**

Bunk Beds • **54**

The Worst Thing About Incest • **55**

Translators' Notes • **57**

Translators' Acknowledgments • **58**

Wendy Guerra lives between worlds. While her poetry and prose can be defined as distinctly Cuban and Caribbean, they capture the nuances of both the colony and the colonists, old and new. Guerra, who grew up under a Communist regime, is not afraid to bring a fresh perspective to the Cuban experience, both on a political and personal level. For example, "On How the Russians Started Saying Goodbye" describes the interaction between the local Cuban community and the Russian soldiers during the Russian presence long after the Revolution. In these lines, Guerra captures the lack of comprehension between both cultures:

> They never fit in
> when they spoke to us we answered dancing
> they never belonged
> [...]
> I remember teaching my friends from Moscow how to beat each
>   other up without crying

Her poetry comprises themes of isolation that are prevalent in immigrant writing and is further intensified by her lived experience. Writing about her native Cuba while living there and confronting the realities of a political system that does not celebrate artistic freedom, Guerra has been a bold and independent voice. Her poetry of transgression and unabashed sexuality was considered controversial by the Cuban government and its supporters. It is not surprising that most of her work has been published abroad—particularly in Spain. In "Breaking Crystal Dragonflies," Guerra writes:

> I already know they are reading my Diaries but I take them with
>   me I write from memory
> They dig their hands into my delicates as if touching my sex they
>   violate my word they silence it

Delicates, our translation of *Ropa interior* (Bruguera, 2009), has taken thirteen years to complete. Esperanza came across the book during a trip to Bogotá in 2010, and began her collaboration with Nancy in 2020. As readers we were drawn to the strong and sensual, yet vulnerable woman's voice infusing the poems, reminiscent of the work of Anaïs Nin. Indeed, Guerra quotes from her letters in the epigraph of this volume, and even describes herself as "a sort of descendant of Nïn."

Although choosing an apt title for this translation did not take us thirteen years, we struggled to find something that would be more evocative than "Underwear," the literal counterpart, and would do justice to representing a balance between Guerra's stark Cuban upbringing and the trends she encountered in her travels across Paris, Spain, and New York. We played with splitting the term into two words ("Under Wear") for enhanced connotation, and even tried "Undergarments" ("Under Garments"), as well as "Unmentionables." We also considered "Dirty Laundry" and "Dirty Linen," but all of these failed to capture the sensuousness of Guerra's compositions. With "Intimates," we got closer to the sensorial effect of the original, and finally landed on "Delicates," which we felt was most accurate.

Translating this book has been a reward and a challenge as Guerra chooses unexpected contexts to set her poems, which in turn become metaphors for her plethora of themes, including the complex dichotomies of love and loss, faith and skepticism, belonging and exile. In "Touché," for example, she uses the sport and art of fencing to address the lover, teasing the reader by saying they are "related by blood," thereby foreshadowing the concluding poem where incest is established as a parallel metaphorical framing. Other striking examples are that of the ruins of Pompeii ("From Pompeii"):

> Good thing I made love to you with my back turned   face down
> and slept in your golden volcano fountain and gave you figs
> in the mouth
> because it was never easy to flee Pompeii.

or a bull ring ("Red"):

I sense in your Cuban voice that pain will always return

I'm trembling but it will always return and won't do any good

It's a bull bleeding in my memories

Several rehearsals to die in the ring

Red

Red

Red and so purple I die.

Music infuses these poems, with a subtle texture of assonance, alliteration, and silence. Indeed, music itself becomes a metaphor, as in "Jazz Trio: Trumpet":

I can't lean on the night without weeping

The trumpet sounds like something lost

That thing you didn't know you were still waiting for.

At the heart of this collection is Cuba, often overtly referenced, as in "Peninsular Psalm," which invokes the sea separating the island country from the rest of the world. Although Guerra uses only one word in Latin, *Marenostrum*, she places it at the beginning and repeats it like a refrain. Inspired by the structure of Biblical psalms, the poet addresses the sea as a believer would address God. The lines that follow offer praise to something greater than our selves:

Marenostrum

you who stretch to where the limit cannot kiss

who make of fish the purest food for humankind

you who sustain ships and worlds

who make an offering of saints to the wind's violent tenderness like
    miracles of faith

you who divide and distance isolate and drive away postpone and
    flee

We can never forget these poems are a prayer for Cuba, woven by someone whose relationship with her native land, her faith, and her country are multi-layered, much like her feelings about men and relationships. The poem "On Your Knees" presents a different spiritual point of view from that of the previous poem. It refers to Santeria, a pantheistic Afro-Cuban religion, while criticizing the church. Guerra opens with a provocative line: "Playing with heads doesn't elevate your soul" and continues in the same ironic vein:

Only tarnished faith looms menacingly
Obeying dark orders
Judging without following the commandments
Preaching misfortune like Peter and the wolf
It's good for the soul to tithe   tithe in a discreet and private way

Delicates informs the reader of what it means to be a woman and an artist in a society that places restrictions on both identities. The speaker in "Red" bemoans her lot:

I am a teardrop lost in the ponds
who no longer returns to the burning red notebook
or the delirium it lights in your desires
I arrive too late to my own redemption among the verses

Guerra's masterful verses open doors to a new way of understanding the lived past and the evolving present of a practicing artist. Her authorial voice invites us readers to live, sing, and suffer along, and be forever changed.

As two women translating a woman poet, we are delighted to be contributing to the greater effort of bringing more women and non-binary writers to the English readership, as well as celebrating world literature and the craft of poetry.

Delicates

Peninsular Psalm

Marenostrum
you who stretch to where the limit cannot kiss
who make of fish the purest food for humankind
you who sustain ships and worlds
who make an offering of saints to the wind's violent tenderness like miracles of faith
you who divide and distance   isolate and drive away   postpone and flee
O, *Marenostrum*!
Just as you have that strength in my past
shatter the crystalline water and cause it to burst forth to heal my tormented present
without fearing the broken waves   *Marenostrum*
and with the conviction of the Messiah on the water   approach me
protect his mysterious entry into my pocket bay
as the river enters its children's eyes
as its mouth enters my small mouth of salt and sand sifted by pain
Marenostrum insular platform   make him take the route of goodness
blue-blood passage through my scattered country   my wounded paradise   my
     etching
make of my body a glass bridge that I may bring home dissipated creatures
illuminate their feet   their course   their footsteps
if they were once my friends never convert them into my enemies   let them come
navigate my sea without judging the communion of our distanced bodies
may their legs' destiny and their eyes' pleasure over the valley
be blessed by your blue
Marenostrum
make them return and do not close the common door which these days remains sealed
so the pleasure of what is not only ours may finally be divine
so you may be sea   man and woman   in the precise humidity of our bodies

so the beach and its surroundings may be yours
so the route fish take through their usurped territory makes sense once more
so we may be together as always and forever more
Amen.

Red

A thousand red flamingos ignited my body on the beaches
Once again sandalwood venom in my scattered mouth
You transform the everyday like winter changes water
From ice to humidity there's scarcely a shiver
A restored song   so many doubts and past grudges
A summer   a season that spills uninterrupted
I am a teardrop lost in the ponds
who no longer returns to the burning red notebook
or the delirium it lights in your desire
I arrive too late to my own redemption among the verses
You pose for the world   but you don't pose for me
Saying goodbye to the fire you leave my coat behind
in a winter so raw I get sick
I sense in your Cuban voice that pain will always return
I'm trembling   but it will always return and won't do any good
It's a bull bleeding in my memories
Several rehearsals to die in the ring
Red
Red
Red and so purple I die.

Snow in Havana

I descend from the misty heavens
in white flakes of iridescent snow

Julián del Casal

Under the blanket the remains of my virginity shipwreck
purity and doubt
Havana dawns   slightly cooler than my eyes
A snow toy for the devious girl
who goes to school disguised as the devil
You've left abandonment confused   the city dead
I carry on in the empty streets
and no longer wait for you because it's very late
And even though it may seem strange   we are alive in the usual zoo
I've discovered myself anchored in the epistolary fiesta of your lies.
I recover the inspiration of my longhand and now narrate the landscape
excluding you
only in loss does one find what was hoped for
a mollusk and a slab of gannet frozen by the ice
I plunge my body into the beach's clairvoyance
and shatter the paralysis of fear *en pointe*
A snow-covered pier   a space flooded with doubt

I write letters in the ardor of time
and discover myself in a luminary drawing
I shatter the paralysis of my stanzas
Now I can only find you skiing
From the deep Caribbean without any news
I float on a profound misunderstanding of snow in my own city
under my own skirt

I wait for the sun since rowing is no longer possible
I cut my hands sliding on the white
A port is an exit to the world   not an ice rink
A stay dislocated in winters
A new labyrinth that I learn and forget
If I now attempt to die under the snow
Havana saves me from the void.

Winter Sports

Flung into fleece   capsized in the best painless libations
Surrendered to the lethargy of bedrock piercing us like an arrow
Up and down the other's body   in perfect dives   suspended
Spilled onto our backs and our knees sweating all the murmur once promised to the sea
Among the drunkenness of some ancient wonders that drank vintage feelings
And from my natural intoxication commending your spell   this is how we winter in the
      tropics
Uncorking everything   open as those who believe in a January summer
Undressing what the confused and distant cold thought could not be bared
That's how you shattered the ice   that's how we reached rock bottom   skiing
      unprotected in the secret Antarctica
Winter sports
Snow games I never knew until I swallowed yours
Hunt ending in a hunger of wild beasts   pulled by sleds   me dragged by your sex
Without a winner other than my body protected by your body
Winter sports in which we are
The glory of our own molten territories.

Salt

I'm on the island   the chasm of the white mountain
I've come to the salt flats to taste the pink in stones on your behalf
The magnitude of acidity in this accident that will never season pain
They suppress the accent of flavors in my supper
They don't add salt so I'll forget
This bitter distance can turn sweet
if it's spilled out backwards on the tablecloth and everything begins again
But it's only salt
and I'll see you one last time
in insomnia.

Traveling in Reverse

I pack and unpack my bags
do and redo everything   planning to leave
I call my friends   I tell them I'm breaking free
then discreetly climb onto the raft
to peacefully soak up the sun's sorceries
A wedding ring lost in the belly of a fish
And once again suitcases for the trip that can't be postponed
I see and see that frozen slab of marble
which becomes the boots of my personal monument
Look how my tears travel on the suitcase
follow them with your index finger
and you will reach the center of my doubts
I fish in the same sea that makes my eyes overflow
I see how my half-packed suitcase rises to the surface
my tormented compass
and a boy's drawing of the Cuban map
I trace the thousand ways of an exploratory survey
Dip your foot in   to test the exact temperature of the waters
pull back a bit   and then leave
for the endless and closing regatta
Someone jokingly shoves me and I almost drown
but I maintain a surprising state of equilibrium
I travel into the interior
enlightened   sighting from afar that I dictate
the last line of my ideas.

A Face in the Crowd (Graffiti)

My parents were once of sound mind
Singing in chorus   they met in a crowded plaza
And loved each other in a sea of ten bunk beds hushed into silence by a voice
They brought me into the world in a room filled with cots   ordered in shared emotions
We swam at beaches packed with bathers blending together in identical
      swimsuits and collective trucks
Saturday nights we watched the same movies
weeping along with a country subtitled in black-and-white
Sundays we said our goodbyes
indistinct in the uniformed   blue that split us apart
My parents   when finally left to themselves
lost their minds.

Memory and Dust

For Mama, Albis Torres

> Your time is now a butterfly,
> a small white vessel, slender, nervous.
>
> S.R.

I humanize the movement of a lost butterfly
fluttering in the epistolary sob of what begins
erasing the ink from the crazed notebook
telling lies about the never-ending wind
and sketching calm while waiting for the breeze
A summer halo arrived drowning pride
and in the pain that agony recalls
she flies violet and strange
As though her state of pregnant beauty were invisible
she falls naked at my feet   without blushing
While I recover dust from her books
she leaves me behind and escapes
between her wings
memory.

News from the Queen

You can't see me
I can't see you or touch you
You can't move from your center but my desire transports you
You're trapped between duty and my entreaties
I'm Juana la Loca and I frolic in the fire of my entelechies
I run around the castle honoring your name
Hair loose and world exposed without knowing   unaware of where they hide you
Who am I   why do I seek you to undress me even as I repent.
To what heights do you transport me   blindfolded
What reasons cause me to die in silence for your honor.

Closed Season on Manatees

We were floating on the golden sunset
gliding the tablecloth's corner along the beach
we buried some belongings and were born
counting pennies like the poor

Salt was sprinkled like snow
and sugar spilled onto newspapers
The wedding ring was lost on the ground
and I found the manatee in the sand
an exotic revelation my body divined
I made up the manatee as a miracle
To swap rings for ideas
money for ghosts
old belongings saved from danger
until reaching the level of living things
I planned to swim long distances
leave the shore and return my inheritance to the rhythmic ocean depths

A manatee holds me up from the bottom
destroys the bathyscaphe so as not to think
I wait for you while caring for my knees smashed by fish
and the head stolen during the closed season

A manatee is drowning between my legs

I am a keeper of a humid and broken zoo
I can't let the manatee die
Gravity and sex in him
weightlessness and magic spells in me

Only a trace in balance with my name
an offering above the sleeping sunset
a sad prayer
a lie floating in gilt
I've given back the gem
I've gifted an ivory umbrella
I've come back to the beach
don't touch me   it's dangerous
I'm closed for the season
I've resolved to be simply a sleeping manatee.

Inuit Promise

For you I will leave the snow   and ski on the sand
I will not write graffiti on the ice
I'll adopt a western accent and summer clothes
my teeth will not tenderize any skin but yours
my scent dissolves in your clean lavender
just like the sturgeon loses caviar I'll lose my name
I'll forget the ritual of the igloo woman and the prey
I'll look upon thawing as water from my sex
at the end of the night I won't give away to strangers what belongs to you
but will stay in your bed provoking fire
and wipe away bait and fish from my mouth
set the sled dogs free
try to forget being exiled from ice
we'll winter together while winter still aches
on the edge of the iceberg   traveling on the white island
my mother's frozen tear
and your father's imploring murmur survive
perhaps amnesia is the best option
even if all appears to belong in another world
together we'll hunt
Inuit promise.

Vertigo Over the Niagara

It's not the first time I straighten Pisa   the proud and falsely inclined tower
meaning to drown me and I won't stand for it
I recover my breath and right the tower
From my vantage point I center it inside my body   Hood of faith protecting me
Yet I keep that structure intact   we are the same leaning towers
If you lie down on the humid grass you will see us seductresses sway in the
blurry photographs
It's Holy Week   everyone races golden bicycles over my back
pedaling and singing to come to my aid
They save the violet girl from the metal-gray danger   cruel gray   unchartered
smudged gray
I want to see the world before I meet my children
I don't know if the vapors above the Niagara are good for a woman with vertigo
The Niagara is   at least a prophetic precipice
Pisa returns to where it belongs   It obeys me
Its spinal column incorporates my balance
Vertigo is   a unique exercise to return to the center
The Niagara   rendezvous for the traveler who misses upright palm trees   their
towers
its starry abysses so high and so impossible.

Delicates

In the showers of men we leave our bodies
tied well to the solar pipes
We mark our territory like animals in heat
our panties saturated with sand and a sidereal isolating odor
Remains of the sex we had yesterday left behind in bathrooms
rose water and wax drippings from vanilla-scented candles
Broken tears in the profane lace of dawn
My earrings have disappeared   lost in the soap of a brief lust
and Sir   the creams anoint your sheets   like venom from silvered goddesses
Look how we snatch freedom from their minds
We open blame under the expanded umbrella of the afternoon
We return with their children withholding the real names of their genes
In delicates we read our pages pursuing only their desire
each line of rice is a moan
Can I hide under my hats   without being found?
Can they guess?
A tunic and a shield that would dodge love's blows
There is more under the hat   I swear
On the bed I assemble the puzzle of words
a white planar surface for skating in the nude   black delicates without pain
and even if I say it all   it would not reach your senses intact
You don't understand   You would have to learn to undress me
We leave the anthropology of a grievous colonization
a colonization close to this weak culture   strong   insecure   exiled sex
I read the lines the editor underscores but don't smoke
I can't allay my anxiety   and can no longer forget what I have lived
In your bathroom still linger my potions   my essences   my slipstream   my stampede
I keep a train   a calla lily   a dragonfly

and the picture of my back taken while I slept
I'm not lace   nor seashell nor evil
it's not only what you see   because I've left
My ideas are more profound than the backs you see in museums
I am my writing and what I try to hide that might not survive
delicates in another bathroom's bottle   another humidity   so much cold
Coats don't exist   they are given away to the other woman I was in an unconnected ritual
there's no snow in this country and even if I were to break down and eternally weep
Only in delicates   do I manage to save myself
I leave my writings in your house but there's more
more frivolous and profound   more pagan
I write on mirrors and you find yourself
swimming in this false oblivion
You snooping inside my handbag
diving into the past like a boy
You only see:
childhood photos with my mother.

Breaking Crystal Dragonflies

I placed your broken dragonfly at the bottom of my empty suitcase
Then blankets and socks for this absurd cold in spring
I already know they are reading my Diaries   but I take them with me   I write
    from memory
They dig their hands into my delicates as if touching my sex   they violate my
    word   silence it
As if breaking dragonflies   they inspect my garments   turn my past upsidedown
You don't walk by   nor enter   nor go to your house   hello and goodbye   already
    your house is not yours
I ask permission to show my naked body in the drawings   it's me on paper
The glass of my tears   Cuba under my skirt
You doubt against the light   breaking   wings stripped from dragonflies
Excess weight of ideas   hidden possessions I don't want to declare without my
    soul   I'm terrified
The books of the dead that I take to survive
Those alive I miss when I read their hands on the damp paper.
Originals   anchors   algae   black records making me surface from the feeling
    of drowning
At the bottom of things some ripe smuggled mangoes   fragrant   incriminating
Sand from Santa María and a virgin who safeguards arrival floating without pain
Wings flapping   this broken dragonfly   this unkempt Cuban woman
    attempts to put her island in the world   the broken endless trip
    in the bottomless suitcase.

Kaos Is Written with a K

After we do drugs it's the moon
after hunger in the flight
then the shakes and flushed faces
the revenge of a luxurious death
neurotic and infinite tower dragging me
you pay for my steps and books
buy me eyeglasses and jewelry
Kaotically occult our knots
the boat maintains its balance
with the night
if all three of us swim over my dress
who's undressing whom
the oars still search for the floating Sioux map
you keep lounging on the same dirty bunk bed
while I can't find the flag on the grass
You count the diamonds in the MoMA
but it's the same cursed vertical bunk bed
we haven't left the cupolas
the school whispers lust to us
while Kaos hunts us down
the cows weep
Mar—a portion of colorful and deep water
Tina—an enormous tub for submerging oneself
Martina has left something for you
In the snow there's a nest in the nest there's an egg
in the egg there's a bird in the bird a worm
in the worm a needle in the needle I leave you the sky

Everywhere your name
hunts me down
tending to the unstable storm
on the boat I leave you my bones
and pull away in the regatta of pain
observing
how Cuba looks like a scrawl
Kaos is written with a K.

The Actress

I'm telling lies
It's all in my head and I make it up
I live in the altarpiece of a country posing for the planet
A country posing and complaining
A country pondering in Latin and speaking in noises   jokes   desire
You threw the javelin flying above my head
I travel with it in countries left out of the official story
You'll never be able to recognize the dark eyes you're already forgetting
Too much obsession over the Water Polo Player
I try to forget that Hockney's swimming pool is real
I'm telling lies
I perform while writing
I look at photographers passing through
I smile and already belong to history
The black-and-white photo of what we have been
Here you have me
Telling lies while I wait for you.

Naughty Girl

They don't read my verses they only look at my hats and begin to ruminate.
I lose the satin mask on airplanes I desire desire desire desire
I want to see myself naked in the face of death
Only my eyes quietly sketch the panic of being
A hat traveling alone among three hundred and fifty terrified passengers
I pee on their computers and they don't know
Luminary humidity birthed among my divine odors
I've discovered they haven't read my verses
I've discovered at last the void
They're unfamiliar with my words just like they don't know my black interior
The word is a dreadful channel leading to mystery
Like doubt that brings the imaginary wake of forgiveness
Over a violated teardrop at last we land
The frivolous opinion of hats sufficed to kill the naked king
But in Havana I'm exposed like a teenage mummy
Like a diamond dissolved in red wine
Like a painting stolen and stolen from a naughty girl's innocence.

Ideas for Silhouettes

Ana Mendieta

"Made of nails
loads of nails
with glass—flecks of white glass—
or broken mirrors"
with all that may ache or calm
in what refracts that pain
so it may return to me without fear
made of fugacious materials
joining reversing that pain
uprooting and escape
in pleasure settling pure
and leaving you in the place before
flight
projected insertion into the promised land
a better idea
made by hand out of nail and glass
finally exorcised
from me.

Last Apocrypha of Ana Mendieta

> I've hurled myself into the same
> elements that produced me, using the
> the earth as my canvas and my soul as
> my tools.
>
> A.M.

Soon   he will make me lean over the balcony to see the world
I taste the cruel transparency of violet   concealed in intense vertigo
Real life   the pain of others from above smells like a rain-soaked street
Leave the earth, pull Cuba out of you or bury yourself completely
If I smash the glass of this aquarium the weight will kill my wayward spirit
My suffering   my fear and the peace this harmony brings   can leave me unpunished.
The sky at last   Have I in fact been beautiful?
They will not deceive me near the end   it would be so cruel to tell lies at this stage
What they expect from me will happen precisely in the air
References for another language
References for a life without relief
Sheets   blood and a mutual desire
To play like girls performing with death
I'll leave flying from his hand   his strength will run out   his patience   his calm   his
    composure
In the precise note that saves us
He will force me to rise from what weighs me down
Nothing there to support this secret Havana–New York bridge
Nothing to hold me in the air should he throw me off
Toccata and fugue in   No   with a dry sound
To the ground in a stampede   with no changes in the drawing's collapse
My clothes moan composing the broken night of wings

Wings of a white chicken   torn to launch my farewell
A flickering light   a strange birthing   a requiem for no one
And even if he wasn't thinking of pushing me
I could hurl myself
I'd have the perfect time in the air to see what I want
Like an intervention in the void
The photo and a silent reconstruction of certain sentiments.

Possible Similes

I'm in front of the face of the black slave   oil on canvas
Velázquez painted it for me   centuries ago just for me   specifically
I've realized you don't need to buy something to own it completely
I have the distinct   feeling that I am and have been your slave for all these years
I have been that indelible mark that never stops serving you
bowing her head and smoothing her hooves in front of you
cheering you on from the grandstand   obediently
I'm that docile horse saving water for the desert
not complaining or grumbling out of fear
that animal, careful not to lose the sure path of a tedious cell
I stand in front of the cold and illuminated museographic act
of an original that puts up with us
I don't feel anything more than the varnish of this era
because I am that slave and I preserve it all
I'll never stop being so   even after centuries
even if scared I run for my life in the storm
even if I were to leave the Met and go down its steps
I'm caught in similes
Don't think returning is liberating oneself   No
Returning is worse   it means staying imprisoned between those awful possibilities
and black similes.

Subway Map

This is the line you must take to find him
you must take this one to come back to me
no confusing the lines   please
white is white and red is red
by going past the old squares you come to me
by stepping inside museums and cafés you'll run into him
Take everything he gives you   except poison
never tell him what you've felt
the word exile is forbidden
don't be a lunatic   don't get naked
don't let him photograph you for nostalgia's sake
don't discuss Havana   don't heal him
don't sing anything which might recall that sound
don't give your book away   don't show him his verse
don't listen to him speak   forget him
don't carry his name in your diary
just get the map and come down to me
finally say goodbye to his reprisals
Once and for all both of you end this silence.

Promenade through the Private Museum

When I abandon, when I leave, when I give up I allow myself to go
forever
a lock of my hair remains tied to the past
tangled in the wires of a minefield
I isolate and punish myself
blood on the mirrors, braid of nightmares and violent mysteries, violated
glass that makes me run away desperate, driving hurt into my feet
forever
a man spies on me between his screams while on my knees I beg for the blueprint
   of the house
lost
locked away in names I recognize
methylene blue, orange villages, purge and pain of pains
which was the first home of blows, was there a home, was there any rest for this
   profound dread
when I abandon, drawers of sand remain
fine dust of a defeated butterfly in my bed
gold on my hands
emptiness between my eyes
from stretcher to stretcher attempting to get nowhere
fever over the body of a queen who'll be cremated because laid bare
arouses pity.

Orgy of the Wind

You contain the wind
You stir all the strange meanings of words
and paintings

I'm not wired to understand
I feel and that hurts
Moored boats emerge under my legs

I watch how a kleptomaniac touches humid gold
he numbs me wearing cold silk gloves
A game of strange hands and legs
While he steals between the two of us   I taste you
You contain light and red wine
I sweat in a winter of fire

I switch to another man   another and another who plays with my skirts
It's the wind   the wind   transparency and scent
white letters dispersed in desire's amorality.

Jazz Trio

TRUMPET

The mute quiets   Calming this neurosis little by little
Lips are figs squeezing the mouthpiece
While the city is a diamond drowned in red wine
The trumpet suffers from what my body feels
It's already very late and the trumpet complains about   all who sleep
Safe from acute pain
I can't lean on the night without weeping
The trumpet sounds like something lost
That thing you didn't know you were still waiting for.

BASS

I step on the club's carpets which tamp down that intense sound
Low   low   low
My clothes plucked in pizzicato get ruined   go slack at the end of the day
Like taut garters they easily pop, defeated
I break free of everything   even when the rhythm of this hour sets the beat
You solemnly play the fibers of my stomach
Now I must surrender to the depth of the sounds
A silvered, moody and humid hour is what remains
Where one plays   in a well-tempered key   the most serious thing is said
Underground   irascible and cunning
That instrument plays dirty with me
It touches what's musty in me and the wooden sound drives me mad.

PIANO

From Russia
From Vienna
From   the Carpathian Mountains
From what faraway place does George Sand come fleeing on her horse
Pursued by two insane pianists   unraveled in her books   Unleashed
She escapes but the sound hovers   harasses her in her obsession
An elephant was slaughtered for the sake of the ivory the finger strokes
An arrangement of white your hands suggest as opposed to ebony
From where does the sound come in crowded rooms
Who renounced their velvet shawl   red from sorrow
Abandoning this ancestral desolation breaking through   in a fugue
The moment the piano tightens its strings   moans   I surrender
What can I do to console it   Nothing

Huge   antediluvian   immovable   inspired and beautiful
From Nigeria
From Abyssinia
From Senegal
From where does this terrifying echo come   so strange.

The Prince and the Pauper

The years have passed and no effort has made this strange creature rave
A secret force lifted me from the mud   the swamp didn't swallow the pearls
And when I thought the kingdom wouldn't reach my hands
when the night closed in on my humid nacreous feet and transparent wounds
a mouse escaped from my torn coat
A coin in my hat transformed alms into a blessing
and the pauper healed the prince from that   pitiless palace vertigo
and the prince healed the pauper from destitution, rescuing him from the cold-exposed
    entrance
The years have passed   I know   what a wonder
We are the same prince and pauper
We own the same tunic and have no greater power than this desire
this private fire which melds us and makes us female and male at the same time
I've already known it
Power and pain have a woman's eyes and legs.

The Year It Snows

for Cousin Olga

> Out of a world we experience from a
> transparent distance, it follows that her
> self-awareness may also be imprecise . . .
>
> Emilio Ichikawa

I attempt to solve the puzzle of an unconventional woman
I don't want to march   and yet I dance
uniformed in my own grief I expect
much more from my heroes than from me
Among the wool socks   Che
the photo recalling the boyfriend of all my girlfriends
It's been impossible to start over even if you escape
the solitary star hangs from your eye with a tear
of bulletproof glass   weep.
The urge to travel will be fierce   but returning is impossible
water separates you from what's close   delays and holds you back
Now distance makes you unique and strange
You attempt to be one more woman lost at Christmas
The city swallows you among the dogs
Dinosaurs from nightmares desert you
You'll come back when snow falls on the impossible
A freezing rain over San Lázaro and Zanja
Virtudes and Villegas
Aguacate and Empedrado
Jovellar and Marina
A white rain separates us
And it's the snow.

Airport

Perhaps I only came to tell you goodbye
To make excuses for losing Paris so far away
I couldn't understand that trip   my constant sobbing
for my own absence
I came to mourn everything I would miss feeling
after leaving
I showed up like a bird beating its wings against the glass
I remained like that   protecting myself from the void   constantly telling you goodbye
A stampede of hellos and goodbyes
Squeezing the umbilical cord that used to tie us to my sex
Letting go of my love like accounts wasted before your eyes
I only came to bid you farewell   It couldn't be helped
I only came to see how I said goodbye to you
I couldn't avoid what I guessed   I didn't know how to alight without a past
Contained by the narrow longitude of our time together   I lost myself
I'm of that race suspending living just from thinking about what we have left
I was once a girl with suitcases and a red beret
A frozen tear in my glory and great fear
Look at me   I didn't have time to tell you what I really came to say
I was only the broken person you saw among the passengers
Telling you goodbye   imprisoned between the glass and her tears.

From Pompeii

I made love to you with my back turned   face down
inside the fountain of the golden volcano   foreshortened
I opened my blouse and offered you figs with my mouth
my legs around your neck and my sex engraved over the text
ashes in my hair   substances spilled on the fire
the island is burning and I remain a prisoner
Good thing I made love to you with my back turned   face down
and slept in your golden volcano fountain and gave you figs
in the mouth
because it was never easy to flee Pompeii.

Far Away Like Cuba

Exposed and foreign among the palm fronds

In a diatribe against the simplest things

Misunderstood and alone   a thousand times alone   in the middle of that ocean
of people drowning with desire

Far away and stubborn like the woman who longs to run toward your embrace
naked and separate

My back turned away from your absence

Reclaiming you in your white-linen paradise

White flag, my love   white flag

Running to avoid colliding into you and stumbling on the map of your eyes   of
my body

Far away like Cuba   Without council

Between the waves making me small and silvered

With the wind against my full sails   I resist weeping

Searching for the naming of a witness   a pilgrim   a sovereign

A creature inside me defending herself

Far away like Cuba

Free island spilled between your legs

Sifting miracles you don't expect

The last bastion of absence

Far away like Cuba   Nearing your salvation

Brief in the north   voluptuous in the south

Asleep without your name   Haunted

With the compass set for one pole and wings watchful at your feet

Waiting for you   with all my roots of land and light

Without that painful tear of goodbye
Here you have me
Far away like Cuba.

Curatorship

I'm a good work of art
Perhaps the best in their complete collection
But so impermanent the MoMA can't preserve me.

Vertical Psalm

Thread of mine
thin string
without obligations without ties not bothersome won't touch you
without intentions without accents without fear without bursting into miracles

Thread of water
thread from the sky
bring me to him
map
of
ice

Thread of everything
thread of mine
let me see him
do it for you.

On Your Knees

"Mayeya, / I don't want you to trick me, respect the *collares*, / don't play around with the saints. // Don't try to trick me with that story, / because everyone in Little Cuba knows one another" . . . "The one not wearing yellow covers up in blue" . . . "Come on, *oribaba* . . . // You shouldn't play in front of the saints . . ."

Ignacio Piñeiro

Playing with heads doesn't elevate your soul
Everything is public and suspect
Necromancy and rumor end
Only tarnished faith looms menacingly
Obeying dark orders
Judging without following the commandments
Preaching misfortune like Peter and the wolf
It's good for the soul to tithe   tithe in a discreet and private way
Delivering prayers to God and in exchange
On your knees
Neither coins   nor fame   nor impossible ties
While you betray and give the saints a makeover
While you traffic in deities
Your body grows old and the spirit escapes   the stain of your disloyalty becomes evident
On your knees   a little later in the rituals
Under veils
Under skirts
Under shame
Playing with other people's heads
Do you find forgiveness?

Excess Baggage

If they let me take everything I miss
if they let me carry the island and the miracle
I'd have no place where I could return
I wouldn't come back to myself
or memories of you.

Consulted Archives

I've found my photo in the social chronicle from the nineteenth
the camera is strapped to my chest it's raining hard
there my memory in liquid crystal capturing other remembrances
deserted archives explaining
why I love you in a way this misguided and merciless way
as if letters took six months to bring solace and news about you
In a steamboat with a Mediterranean name you arrive
with the shorthand of a nonsensical code I ask you to come back
bundled up I write out of my mind without smoking without doing
    drugs without drama
in the proposal of a broken marriage like the alabaster cup
we didn't buy because we never shared that apartment together
vacant ready to be furnished
Now that it's the twenty-first I don't feel your eyes on my coat
I don't appear in the consulted archives
and no matter how hard I search in the diaries if you're not there, Anaïs,
    then I don't exist.

Without Salvation

Nothing saves you from love
Not pilgrimages to interior cities
Not the gift for prayer
Not intuition
Not a healthy childhood
Not the magic of subjectivity
Not the exception of a clear path before your feet
Not the legacy of impressions
Not letters from friends preaching their faith in the power of the mind
Nothing saves you from love   From what I feel
Not the strongest philosophies with their wholesome drugs
Not doors securely locked in someone else's last name
Not bolts or keys   Victorian locks   chastity belts   nor my body
Not the garden leading to the slippery water of algae
Not the Middle Ages   nor the world I must deal with for having been born in the
    seventies
Nothing saves   from love   Look, I'm searching
Not the bareness of a family tree in the fall   detached from the afternoon
Not the clothes I abandoned without being afraid
Not my retouched dark eyes
Not my hair in the sealed frames in the museums of man
Not growing up   nor laughing   nor doing it and undoing it on the bed like an
    imaginary creature
Nothing saves me from love
There's no possible way   to control for that   mercy doesn't exist
There's no lifeline inside me vigilantly keeping watch
Even if I'd read in today's paper   the best news of my life

I'd go tell him about it like a lost girl   I'd ask for help being   believing to
   be   desire
Because nothing saves   not even love.

A Cabala of Cast-offs

A cup of glass
a prism
a calla lily
a photo of Prague
a cup of rice
the flavor of figs released from the wine
a strange balance between sweet and bitter
I am daughter and sister crushing eyeglasses
I am wrapped in the glow of a very slow boil
without knowing about winter I get naked and tell you
celery over the oil
poison over the heat
salt
airports
milk from a baby's bottle
recorded applause
stir slowly in your delirium
a woman   a letter with a name
a gift from Zaire
an airplane forgotten in the cold sketch
a dish from the devil
an inexplicable nexus between nest and life.

Touché

No one could touch there
like someone cracking the nut
Like slicing life and pulling back
No one could touch there   explore with that intimacy of you tasting me
We are related by blood   an extension of this secret touch
No one before you could know the key to my sex
You remember which country is mine
I find your back from my awakening
Yours is a secret touch and when you get naked
I feel the same sacred touch of your body
tapping on my gagged waist
No one can pull us apart
We are up there
delirious
and New York's out there
waiting.

Razor to the Wind

Someone
always
appears
and tears
my favorite pants
It's always him   the same one   with his razor to the wind   slashing this body
with the blade of my own fear.

Living on the Airwaves

Music dawns in the tea brimming with ants
My mother cuts the truth with scissors   with great care
she sharpens her tongue while reporting on what is taboo
They summon me to a café   through airway-coded messages
There's a list of friends we're not allowed to listen to
And I hum them through a dark corridor leading nowhere
Dawn arrives on the airwaves   outside it rains or it's cold
Radio heroes die
They die in the anonymity of their lost voices
An effect
An old-fashioned sinister echo that still fills me with dread
A lie on the frequency-modulated air
So many tears and so much pain   so much laughter and so much bravado
For the wind to later lift it all away.

On How the Russians Started Saying Goodbye

They never fit in
when they spoke to us we answered dancing
they never belonged
they walked around conspicuous as their smell
mysterious as their submarines
I don't know where I can send them this letter
I remember teaching my friends from Moscow how to beat each other up without
    crying
but they never fit in   perhaps it was the heat or the movies
little by little they started saying goodbye and
*Koniec.**

* "The end" in Russian

Déclassée

I can't be your equal.
My plate of food was different from the cousins'
Morphologically I sprinkle essentials like nouvelle cuisine
My adult mannerisms gave away what I would become
Alone in apartments   reading   while the bicycles were someone else's
and the dolls as cold as buying oneself a child
I can't be what you ask   It wasn't mother and the father was absent
I used to belong to an unofficial world   I didn't show up in statistics or social rankings
I didn't have a famous last name
I don't remember a single birthday cake populated with a single candle
My mother was the diatribe between families
A rebel-shield in the harmony of her archangel hands
She asked the cards which grew silent faced with estrangement
Once again they don't let me through to the next family
Once again a woman from the outside is kept from living among so many old
      people   former acquaintances
Royalty is not an ideal place for this strange girl
Je suis déclassée   c'est la vie
And that's how they'll start letting me in   as they can
I defend myself and don the armor that may protect this pain
The black sheep in the concert hall populated with white animals
Don't ask me to believe in all of you   this is me
Letting in is not accepting   never forget it.

Sea of Tears

I'm doing fine
"between the sea and the wall" on my knees among panes of glass
stepping on my personal belongings   evacuating   saving the soul at all costs
I'm all prayed out and I drown pianos on the shore
attempting to get there   attempting to make up another possible geography
sobbing replaces the insular silence of cyclones
unwillingness to speak ends up being the only visible sin   it's raining gray   Juan Gris
keeping quiet amid the buzzing of silence   no   no   no   no   no   no
years of fear   pain   goodbyes, detachments in B double flat
key by key we sink the advantages of a sustained miracle
if we keep weeping like this the sea will swell and the distance will get worse
deep
insurmountable
endemic   enervated
no need to throw more pearls into the sea
it aches   swells the width
we humor this hopeless latitude
a rain of tears detaches and isolates
each dampened body part makes one weep
I'm doing fine
Shivering among panes of glass   swimming in this   Sea of tears.

Bunk Beds

Look   we tried to put distance between us
To the point of rehearsing being enemies
Look   we won   prizes   money and spaces in museums so far away
Look   you call me from the other side of the world to weep or laugh at my fears
Look   time goes by and I dress and undress without discovering the years
The school has been restored and new faces blend into each other in my wake
How useless the trips
How stupid to distance oneself
How painful this strange thought of erasing
We all keep sleeping on filthy bunk beds
You on top and I underneath   For eternity
Making love   Eating   Defending ourselves from everything
Demystifying the canonical and the classical
Spending winters like one long cumulative head cold
Shivering because of the grades life will give us
Look   we are far from each other but I persist
Asking you to lower the volume on WQAM
To not move so much
To leave me in peace   without the excessive   promiscuity that brought us together
Asleep in the vertical building maintaining us
Subsidized
Connected
Grouped
Quoted
Distinguished
Missing you terribly
Asleep on the bunk bed   sincerely yours I bid you farewell.

The Worst Thing About Incest

Don't fear being my father
Let your blushing show through and let's see each other in that same expression
Don't tremble before my masculine side   the culprit summoning me to be daring
Be open and let the fantasies of my legacy be revealed   without revulsion
Abandon me to search for myself, scavenging through your leftovers
Your handouts on my tattooed back
A few mistakes without public consequences
Don't search in the past of things and now let the light descend upon my forehead
Don't fear being my father   don't rein in desire because of the natural bond
    keeping us apart
We are unique   alienated   unfamiliar   don't blame yourself
Worse is the orphanhood of being kept in the dark
Attempting to find you in my drawings
Or in the naked photos I let strangers take of me
I'm not the judge   or the enemy
I'm the daughter.

Translators' Notes

PAGE 3 | *Marenostrum* is Latin for "our sea."

PAGE 25 | Ana Mendieta (1948–1985) was a Cuban-American artist best known for her performance art and her "Silueta Series." The circumstances under which she fell to her death from a 34th-floor Manhattan apartment remain a mystery.

PAGE 42 | The term *collares* refers to beaded necklaces worn for protection from evil and associated with Santeria, a pantheistic Afro-Cuban religion arising from the Yoruba people. *Oribaba* may refer to the words spoken (most likely from Yoruba) at the start of a song by the Orishas, a Cuban hip-hop group.

Translators' Acknowledgments

We are truly indebted to Naveen Kishore and the editorial team at Seagull Books, including Sayoni Ghosh, for her eagle-eyed edits, and Sunandini Banerjee for her haunting cover design. We also extend our gratitude to those who have supported us with their comments and suggestions as we made our way through the translation, including Jeffrey Levine, Michael Maxwell, Ted Miller, Andrew Motion, and William Snyder. Further thanks are due to *Exchanges: Journal of Literary Translation* for granting us permission to draw from an earlier version of our foreword that was published in their Fall 2021 issue. We are very grateful to the editors of the following literary journals in which these translations first appeared, some in earlier versions:

Bellingham Review: "Far Away Like Cuba," "Living on the Airwaves"

Bennington Review: "Possible Similes"

EcoTheo Review: "Vertical Psalm"

Exchanges: Journal of Literary Translation: "Bunk Beds," "Touché," "The Worst Thing About Incest"

Free State Review: "Closed Season on Manatees," "Kaos Is Written with a K"

The Georgia Review: "Curatorship," "Ideas for Silhouettes," "Last Apocrypha of Ana Mendieta," "Promenade through the Private Museum"

The Gettysburg Review: "The Year It Snows," "Without Salvation"

Gulf Coast: "Bass," "Piano"Without Salvation

Latin American Literature Today: "The Actress," "Inuit Promise," "Memory and Dust," "Orgy of the Wind," "Subway Map"

Mid-American Review: "A Face in the Crowd," "Salt," "Winter Sports"

Notre Dame Review: "Naughty Girl," "Traveling in Reverse"

On the Seawall: "Breaking Crystal Dragonflies," "On How the Russians Started Saying Goodbye," "Red," "Vertigo Over the Niagara"

Poetry Northwest: "Peninsular Psalm," "Traveling in Reverse"

The Southern Review: "Sea of Tears," "Trumpet"

Spoon River Poetry Review: "A Cabala of Cast-offs," "Consulted Archives," "Excess Baggage," "From Pompeii," "The Prince and the Pauper"

Tupelo Quarterly: "Déclassée," "Delicates," "Snow in Havana"